Grades 2-3

Written by Q. L. Pearce
Illustrated by Dana Regan

JOSEPHSON INSTITUTE OF ETHICS SM

TRUSTWORTHINESS • RESPECT
RESPONSIBILITY • FAIRNESS
CARING • CITIZENSHIP

Editor: Hanna Otero
Book Design: Riley Wilkinson
Cover Design: Riley Wilkinson
Pre-Press Production: Carol Arriola, Drew R. Moore

Written by Q.L. Pearce
Illustrated by Dana Regan
Cover Illustration by Dana Regan

Table of contents

introduction

○ ○ ○ ○ ○ ○ ○ ○ ○ ○ ○ ○ ○ ○

by Michael Josephson, President, CHARACTER COUNTS!℠ Coalition

Character is what a person is inside. Our character is revealed by how we act when we think no one else is looking. It is how we treat people who we think cannot help or hurt us. A person of character has good ethical values that distinguish right from wrong and a strong commitment to do what is right even when it is inconvenient, uncomfortable, or personally costly. Character, in short, is moral strength.

Good character does not develop spontaneously. Rather, it is the result of conscientious efforts to instill and reinforce ethical values in a way that makes them second nature. This sense of right and wrong is often referred to as the conscience. Conscience is the moral compass of character.

This book is organized around the Six Pillars of Character℠, a character development framework developed by the CHARACTER COUNTS!℠ Coalition, an alliance of hundreds of leading educational, youth-serving, and community organizations dedicated to strengthening the character of youth. The Six Pillars of Character℠ are trustworthiness, respect, responsibility, fairness, caring, and citizenship.

Spotlight on Character: Plays That Show CHARACTER COUNTS!℠ features seven plays, each with extension activities that focus on a unique pillar of character. Creative dramatics is an exciting way to teach character education. It allows children to acquire knowledge and express their feelings through reading, speaking, movement, singing, and art. It requires teamwork and cooperation as well as individual reflection and initiative.

Effective character education, of course, goes beyond the memorization of words. It involves the inculcation of habits that form internal mechanisms of control and moral courage. Character education is necessary to help students develop the tools and strategies to make moral choices they can be proud of. A teacher can provide no greater gift.

Shinrai the Camel
represents trustworthiness.

Austus the Lion
is full of respect.

Ansvar the Elephant
is very responsible.

Guisto the Giraffe
is a symbol of fairness.

Karina the Kangaroo
is caring.

Kupa the bear
is a good citizen.

Dear Parents,

a child's character forms early and is influenced by experiences and role models in the home, school, community, and media. As adults we share the responsibility to teach, enforce, advocate, and model sound character. With this in mind, our class will soon begin work on a series of plays that focus on character education as part of the national CHARACTER COUNTS!℠ program.

CHARACTER COUNTS!℠ is a nonpartisan, nonsectarian alliance of more than 300 non-profit organizations. National members include American Youth Soccer Organization, Big Brothers Big Sisters of America, Boys and Girls Clubs of America, 4-H, National Association of Professional Educators, National Council of La Raza, Points of Light Foundation, United Way of America, and the YMCA of the United States. Their goal is to strengthen the character of America's youth using a set of common values.

The plays will illustrate and reinforce the Six Pillars of Character℠ central to the CHARACTER COUNTS!℠ program:

Trustworthiness: integrity, honesty, reliability, loyalty, and moral courage

Respect: courtesy, tolerance, regard for the rights of others

Responsibility: accountability, pursuit of excellence, self-control, and resolve

Fairness: justness, impartiality, respect for fair rules

Caring: compassion, kindness, consideration

Citizenship: willingness to work for the good of the community, to be a good neighbor, to respect just laws, to care for the environment

Please feel free to contact me if you have any questions or concerns, or if you would like to assist in the production of the plays.

Sincerely,

setting the stage

○ ○

Overview

Producing a play can be fun for all involved. First, decide if your performance will be a small production for fellow classmates, another class, or parents. If your students would like to invite guests, you might need space in a multipurpose room or auditorium.

If the children are nervous about learning lines, you can suggest a reader's theater. Rather than memorizing the script, the performers give a dramatic reading complete with gestures and movement. An added benefit is that a minimum of rehearsal time is needed, and the play can be performed within a day or two of the first reading. A puppet show is particularly enjoyable for early grades. Shy students often feel more comfortable speaking their lines from behind a puppeteer's curtain.

A stage production offers several variations. You can keep it simple by using an open corner in the classroom as a stage, or have the students perform in the center of the classroom with the audience seated around them. This "theater in the round" eliminates the need for the actors to worry about turning their backs to the audience. If you want to give the impression of a true stage, hang up a large sheet to act as a curtain. Although scenery isn't required, it might be fun for the class to paint a scene on an old sheet to use as a backdrop. Large pieces of cardboard can serve the purpose as well. Such backdrops are easy to paint and can be changed quickly during a performance.

Warming Up

Although many children like to perform, it's a good practice to warm everyone up to the idea first. Here are a few activities that can get the creativity flowing:

Mimic. You'll need a tape player and a variety of musical tapes. Have the students line up on one side of the room and choose a leader. Explain that when the music starts, the leader should strut or march around the room, with the other children following and mimicking his or her performance. Begin with a lively tune. After a minute or two, change the music and the leader. Some children will see it as an opportunity to be silly, but it does break the ice.

Pantomime. Make time for pantomime. Cut a small strip of paper for every student and write the name of an animal, a famous person, or an action on each strip. Place the papers in a box and have each student draw one. He or she must then act out what is written while the class tries to guess what it is.

React. Have the students stand in a circle. Begin by telling them you are going to pass an invisible object around the circle and you want each of them to react to it. Choose something (a snake, an ice cube, a puppy). Pantomime holding it, and then pass it on.

The First Read Through

Now you're ready to introduce the play to your class. Pass out a script to each student. Read the play aloud as they read along silently. Explain how tone can affect the meaning of a sentence. As an example, say a sentence such as *Bring me that bag.* Say it several times. Emphasize a different word each time. Say it fast and nervously, then slow with menace. Once you have made your point, ask individual students to read a few lines from the play.

Assigning Parts

For the leading roles it is best to choose students who are cooperative and show enthusiasm for the undertaking. Balance the cast between outgoing and more reserved students. Your primary goal is to have everyone participate, but the number of parts in each play is limited. Several of the plays offer opportunities to cast by-standers who would like to be on stage but are uncomfortable with speaking parts.

Not all participants must be actors. There are "behind the scenes" jobs for everyone:

- **Understudies** learn and rehearse one or more parts. They perform if another player is absent.

- The **announcer** introduces the play and players to the audience.

- The **stage manager** raises the curtain and is in charge of sound effects and changes of scenery.

- The **property master/costumer** takes care of any props and makes sure that costume requirements are met.

- **Playbill writers** and **illustrators** may create a program for the performance that shows who plays which parts. They may also prepare a poster with the name of the play and players to be placed on an easel near the stage.

Rehearsal

Keep all rehearsals upbeat and reasonably short. For the first rehearsal, have the students do a read-through using the scripts. It will help to have each actor mark his or her part with highlighter. Once the actors are comfortable with their parts, do a walk-through. Use the scripts, but block out some movement for the scene. This is a good time to introduce the concept of stage position. Explain that these positions are from the point of view of the actor facing the audience.

Schedule a little extra rehearsal time for your lead players. When the students are comfortable with their parts, try a rehearsal without scripts while adding in gestures. Your final run-through should be a dress rehearsal with props. Try to let the actors get through the entire play without interruption, as if the audience were already there. Reassure players and crew alike that the purpose of the play is to entertain and have fun.

resources
○ ○○ ○ ○○○○○○○○ ○○

For Adults

Bringing Up a Moral Child: A New Approach for Teaching Your Child to be Kind, Just, and Responsible by Michael Schulman and Eva Mekler (Addison-Wesley, 1985)—Gives parents and teachers ideas for helping children in challenging situations.

The Moral Child: Nurturing Children's Natural Growth by William Damon (The Free Press, 1988)—Suggestions for incorporating moral growth into a child's natural development.

Educating for Character: How Our Schools Can Teach Respect and Responsibility by Thomas Likona (Bantam, 1991)—Guidance for teachers who wish to incorporate character-building into their school programs.

For Students

Trustworthiness

Sam, Bangs & Moonshine by Evaline Ness (Holt, 1967)— Sam is a young girl who regularly stretches the truth. This causes problems for her and her cat Bangs. Highlighted by Caldecott-winning illustrations.

Max Malone and the Great Cereal Rip-Off by Charlotte Herman (Holt, 1990)—Max challenges the makers of his favorite cereal when he discovers the box lacks his expected prize.

The Adventures of Obadiah by Brinton Turkle (Viking, 1988). Obadiah stretches the truth so often that his family doesn't believe him when he tells them about his real experience at the sheep-sheering fair.

Jamaica's Find by Juanita Havill (Houghton Mifflin, 1986). Jamaica finds a stuffed toy that is hard to part with, but when she returns it, she gains a friend.

Video: *Shiloh* (Warner Home Video, 1997)—From the book by Phyllis Reynolds Naylor. A young boy must wrestle with the need for truthfulness and responsibility to help a young dog.

Respect

Smoky Night by Eve Bunting (Harcourt Brace, 1994)— Two cats help to heal a small part of the community during the Los Angeles riots.

Stellaluna by Janelle Cannon (Harcourt Brace Jovanovich, 1993)—A young bat is adopted by a family of birds. Even when Stellaluna learns that he is different from his adopted family, their love endures.

Manners by Aliki (Green Willow, 1990). This book gives a look at manners, good and bad, in many situations.

I Am Rosa Parks by Rosa Parks with Jim Haskins (Dial, 1997). Rosa Parks's autobiographical account of her part in the civil rights movement illustrates the power of peaceful resistance.

Video: *Babe* (MCA/Universal Home Video, 1996)— Based on the novel by Dick King-Smith, this Academy Award-nominated film shows that in spite of superficial differences, kindness and respect prevail.

Responsibility

School's Out by Johanna Hurwitz (William Morrow, 1991)—Lucas thinks that summer vacation means he can leave rules and responsibility behind. When he decides to play pranks on his caretaker, he learns that responsibility doesn't take a vacation.

Brave Irene by William Steig (Farrar, Straus & Giroux, 1986)—In spite of a raging storm, Irene is determined to deliver the dress her mother has made for the Duchess to wear to the ball.

Keep the Lights Burning, Abbie by Peter and Connie Roop (Carolrhoda, 1985). This is the true story of a girl in 1856 who keeps the lighthouse lamps lit during a winter storm.

Video: *The Indian in the Cupboard* (Columbia, Paramount, 1995)—From the book by Lynne Reid Banks. Omri gets a magical gift for his birthday that leads to difficult choices.

Fairness

Teammates by Peter Golenbock (Harcourt Brace Jovanovich, 1990). Jackie Robinson was the first African American to play Major League baseball. When Robinson met with racial prejudice, his white teammate Pee Wee Reese made a dramatic public gesture of support.

The Value of Fairness: The Story of Nellie Bly by Ann Donegan Johnson (Danbury Press, 1977). When Nellie Bly decided to travel around the world and write about it, she was told women couldn't travel alone.

The Stinky Sneakers Contest by Julie Ann Peters (Little, Brown, 1992)—When Damian and Earl compete, Earl usually loses. He doesn't realize that Damian cheats.

Arthur's Pen Pal by Lillian Hoban (Harper & Row, 1976)—Arthur finds a penpal and also learns about fairness.

Caring

The Wednesday Surprise by Eve Bunting (Clarion, 1989)—Anna helps her grandmother prepare a very special surprise for her father's birthday.

Charlotte's Web by E.B. White (Harper, 1952)—Charlotte, Wilbur, Fern, and Templeton show the true meaning of friendship and caring. Charlotte's death is tragic, but her powerful legacy is hope.

A Picture Book of Florence Nightingale by David Adler (Holiday House, 1992). Florence Nightingale dedicated her life to helping the poor and sick. Her work changed the nursing profession.

Mufaro's Beautiful Daughters by John Steptoe (Lothrop, Lee & Shepard, 1987). Mufaro sends his two beautiful daughters—one ill-tempered and one kind—to meet the king, who is looking for a wife.

Video: *The Secret Garden* (Republic Pictures Home Video, 1992)—Based on the book by Frances Hodgson Burnett, first published in 1911. A friendship among three children plants the seeds of hope, courage, and love.

Citizenship

50 Simple Things Kids Can Do to Save the Earth by The Earthworks Group (Andrews & McMeel, 1990)—A cornucopia of ideas that show children that they have the power to do something positive for the planet.

Come Back, Salmon by Molly Cone (Sierra Club, 1992). This book tells the true story of elementary school children who adopted a creek and brought it back to life.

Just a Dream by Chris Van Allsburg (Houghton Mifflin, 1990). Walter doesn't do his part to keep the environment clean, until he has a dream that takes him to the future.

trustworthiness

The Deal

Cast of Characters

Ian A third-grade boy
Rachel Ian's older sister
Mom Ian's mother
Woman A customer at the yard sale
Joseph A friend of Ian
Mario A friend of Joseph
Gary A classmate of Ian
Mrs. Mason Gary's mom

Scene One: Ian's front yard. The family is having a yard sale and there are objects set out, including a skateboard.

Enter Mom, Rachel, and Ian carrying more items.

Mom: That should be everything. Ian, you and Rachel stay here and help anyone who needs it. I'll be at the table over there. *(She points offstage.)*

Rachel: Okay.

Exit Mom.

Ian: Looks like we have our first customer.

Enter woman with baby.

Rachel: *(to woman)* Do you need any help?

Woman: I'm looking for baby clothes.

Rachel: We have some over here. *(They move upstage.)*

Enter Joseph and Mario.

Joseph: Hey, Ian. What's up? Are you guys moving?

Ian: No, my mom just wanted to clear out some things.

Mario: *(picking up skateboard)* You're selling this?

Ian: Yes, I got a new one from my uncle.

Joseph: It's so cool! I would really like to get it. How much are you selling it for?

Ian: Ten dollars.

Mario: That's not bad.

Joseph: I have eight dollars at home. I could give you that and pay you the rest when I get my allowance.

Ian: That sounds okay. It's a deal.

Joseph: All right! I'll go get my money. C'mon, Mario.

Mario: We'll be back in a while.

Exit Joseph and Mario.

Rachel: *(putting something in a plastic bag)* I'm glad you like it.

Woman: It's just what I needed. *(She hands Rachel some money.)*

Rachel: Thank you.

Exit woman.

Rachel: *(to offstage Mom)* Mom, we made our first sale.

Exit Rachel. Enter Gary and Mrs. Mason, Gary's mother. Mrs. Mason moves upstage to look at the things.

Gary: Hi, Ian. What are you guys selling?

Ian: Mostly clothes and stuff.

Gary: *(picking up the skateboard)* Wow, this is great!

Mrs. Mason: *(moving downstage)* Did you find something you like?

Ian: I'm sorry, but I already promised that to someone else for ten dollars. We have a deal.

Enter Rachel.

Mrs. Mason: I'll tell you what. I'll give you fifteen dollars for it. That's an even better deal. We'll take the board over there and Gary can try it out.

Exit Gary and Mrs. Mason carrying board.

Ian: *(to Rachel)* What should I do? I've already promised the board to Joseph, but Gary will give me more money.

Rachel: It's your board. You'll have to decide. Come on. Mom wants us to help her with something.

Exit Rachel and Ian.

Scene Two: Later in Ian's yard. The board is nowhere to be seen.

Enter Ian and Rachel carrying baskets of things. They set them down.

Enter Joseph and Mario.

Joseph: Hey, Ian, I have all the money. My dad gave me the extra two dollars. Where is the skateboard?

Ian: Well . . . *(Pause. He finally smiles and reaches behind a box to pull out the skateboard.)* It's right here. I put it away so no one else would try to buy it.

Joseph: *(handing Ian the money)* Wow! Thanks. I'm really glad you saved it for me.

Ian: *(smiling back and winking at Rachel)* A deal's a deal.

extension activities
for trustworthiness

Definition

On the board, write this definition of trustworthiness:

A trustworthy person does . . .

- tell the truth.
- keep promises.
- stand up for what is right even if it is difficult.

A trustworthy person doesn't . . .

- cheat, steal, or lie.
- spread rumors or gossip.
- tell another person's secrets.

Lead a class discussion on the meaning of each aspect of trustworthiness.

Q & A

Once you have read through the play, ask your students to answer such questions as these:

- Would you have sold the skateboard to Gary instead? Why or why not?
- If Ian made a promise to you, would you believe him?

Things Unsaid

Explain to students that you don't actually have to tell a lie to be dishonest. Sometimes it is enough to knowingly not give all of the information. Offer several situations, such as the following:

- A child doesn't tell his parents where he is really going on his bike and he gets lost.
- A person breaks the leg of a chair but just props it up and doesn't say anything.

Ask how each situation can be harmful.

What Would You Do If . . . ?

Divide the class into five or six groups. Think of a variety of situations such as these:

- You get too much change at the store.
- You find a wallet.
- You break your mom's favorite lamp.
- You don't finish your homework on time.
- You lose a library book.

Give each group a different situation and have the group members work together to create a list of do's and don'ts for each situation. Have each group ask and answer this question: *How would a person of character handle the problem?*

Building Trust

Create a simple obstacle course in your classroom. Place an empty box at one end of the course and have a blindfolded student stand at the other end. Explain that the student will have to trust a classmate to guide him or her through the course to the box. Give each student a chance to be the blindfolded student as well as the guide. Then ask these questions: *How did it feel to have to trust someone so completely? What was it like to be responsible for the safety of another student?*

Not Too Nice to Visit and I Wouldn't Want to Live There

Ask your students to write short stories about a town where no one told the truth. In their stories have them answer these questions: *What would it be like to spend the day in the town? What is the name of the town?*

Mr. President

Tell the class the story of George Washington and the cherry tree. Explain that we don't know if the story really happened, but that it gives us an idea of the kind of person the first president was.

Write this quote on the board:

> I hope I shall always have firmness and virtue enough to maintain what I consider the most enviable of all titles, the character of an "Honest Man."
>
> —George Washington

Lead the class in a discussion of why George Washington felt that honesty was so important.

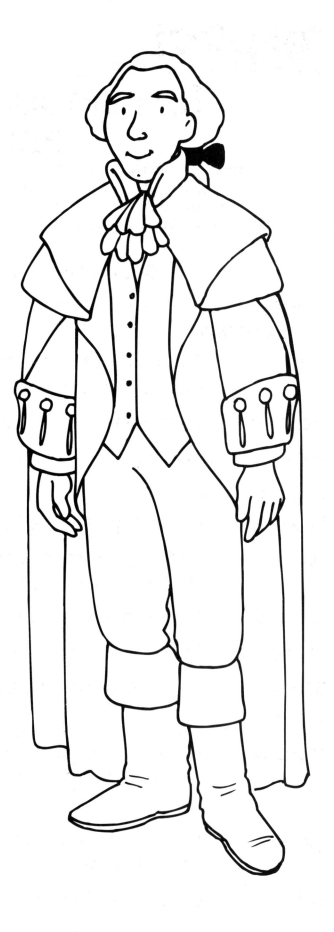

respect

Turnabout Is Fair Play

Cast of Characters

Laura A second-grade girl
Tony Laura's friend
Brooke Laura's classmate
Theresa Julie's friend

Natalie Laura's friend
Ted Laura's friend
Julie Laura's cousin
Wendy Julie's friend

Scene One: The school cafeteria.

Enter Laura, Natalie, Ted, and Tony. They sit down at a table to eat their lunches.

Tony: Oh, man, my dad gave me peanut butter again. Does anybody want to trade?

Natalie: I'll trade you for tuna fish.

Tony: Okay.

Enter Brooke.

Brooke: Hi, you guys. What's going on?

Laura: Nothing. Natalie, are you going to the father-daughter dance next week?

Brooke: Can I sit with you?

Laura: There really isn't enough room. Sorry.

Brooke: Okay, maybe another time.

Exit Brooke.

Natalie: We could have moved over. You're always mean to Brooke. She just wants to be friends. Don't you like her?

Laura: I don't know. I guess she's okay, but I don't need any new friends.

Tony: I think she felt bad.

Laura:	That's not my problem. There are plenty of other places she can sit. Now let's talk about something else. I'm going to visit my cousin Julie this weekend.
Ted:	Where does she live?
Laura:	Not too far, but I haven't seen her in a long time. I think it will be fun.
Tony:	Oh, no, peanut butter cookies. Does anybody want to trade?

Fade.

Scene Two: The park near Julie's house.

Enter Laura and Julie.

Julie:	There are my friends. Hi, Theresa! Hi, Wendy!

Enter Theresa and Wendy.

Theresa:	Hi, Julie! Wait until you see what my dad brought me from his trip. Look. It's the coolest book on the rain forest.
Wendy:	It has all kinds of stuff about some really weird animals.
Laura:	I like the rain forest. *(The girls stop and look at her.)*
Julie:	Oh, this is my cousin, Laura.
Theresa:	Hello. *(Julie, Wendy, and Theresa go back to looking at the book, leaving Laura off to one side.)*
Julie:	Wow, look at that! That must be the biggest snake in the world.
Theresa:	I wouldn't want to run into one of those.
Laura:	*(trying again)* My next-door neighbor has a pet snake.
Wendy:	That's nice. Julie, are you going to go to pizza night on Wednesday? My dad said we could go.
Theresa:	I'll bet we can't. My mom's on a diet. *(Theresa, Julie, and Wendy laugh. Laura watches sadly.)*

Julie:	I'm thirsty. Let's go get a drink of water.

Exit Julie, Theresa, and Wendy. Laura trails after them.

Scene Three: The cafeteria at Laura's school.

Enter Laura, Natalie, Tony, and Ted. They sit at a table.

Tony:	I can't believe this. It's peanut butter again.
Ted:	I'll trade you that for my egg salad sandwich.
Tony:	All right.
Natalie:	So, did you have a nice time at your cousin's house this weekend?
Laura:	Not really. I ended up watching a lot of television by myself.

Enter Brooke. She is looking around for a place to sit.

Laura:	Hey, Brooke. *(Brooke walks over uncertainly.)* We have plenty of room. Why don't you sit with us? Scoot over, Ted.
Brooke:	Thanks. *(She sits down.)*
Laura:	Brooke, are you going to go to the father-daughter dance next week?
Brooke:	Yes, my dad already said it was okay.
Natalie:	Mine, too.
Laura:	Maybe we could all go to my house after school and practice dancing.
Brooke:	That would be fun.
Ted:	I don't want to practice dancing. Yuck.
Natalie:	You don't have to. It's a father-daughter dance.
Tony:	Hey, Brooke, do you like peanut butter?

Fade.

extension activities
○○○○○○○○○○○○○○○○○○○○○○○○○○○
for respect

Definition

On the board, write this definition of respect:

A respectful person . . .

- treats others as he or she would like to be treated.
- accepts others for who they are, not for what they look like or what they have.
- respects the privacy, freedom, and property of others.
- tries to understand different points of view.
- is polite and courteous.

A respectful person doesn't . . .

- use insults or bad language.
- use physical force to settle disagreements.
- make fun of or embarrass others.

Lead a class discussion on the meaning of each aspect of respect.

Q & A

Once you have read through the play, ask your students such questions as these:

- How do you think Laura felt when she was ignored by her cousin's friends?
- Did Julie treat Laura respectfully?
- Why do you think Laura treated Brooke differently at the end of the play?

The Golden Rule

Write the Golden Rule on the chalkboard: *Do unto others as you would have them do unto you.* Lead a discussion on the meaning of the rule. Ask your students if the rules applies exclusively to people. Should we use it as a guide when dealing with animals as well?

Role Models

Ask each student to choose a person he or she respects and write a short paragraph about the person. Instruct the students to include the reason why they respect the people they chose.

Showing Respect

Write these words across the chalkboard: *parents, friends, the environment, teachers, self, country.* Explain to the students that these are all people or things that generally deserve respect. Ask them if they would like to add to the list. Then challenge the students to think of ways that they can show respect to each of the people and things listed. Write the responses on the chalkboard.

What a Bore

Ask each student to write a paragraph about a town where everyone is exactly the same. Have the students answer these questions as they write:

• Would it be an interesting place to live?

• What would be some of the drawbacks?

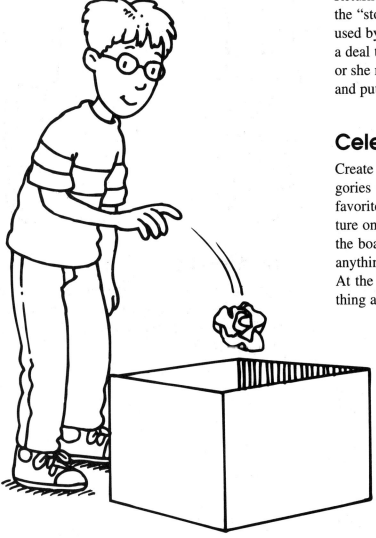

A Wonderful World

Make a bulletin board of people of all races and cultures doing similar things. Choose a theme, such as weddings, birthday celebrations, or family dinners to show that people all over the world do the same things but in different ways. Ask your students to share some of their own family traditions.

Sticks and Stones

Remind the class of this old rhyme: Sticks and stones will break my bones, but names will never hurt me. Ask your students if they think the saying is true. Ask if name-calling can be hurtful. Then give each child a square of paper and ask him or her to write on it a name or word that he or she thinks is hurtful. Have the students crumple up the papers to make "stones" and put them in a box. Read one or two of the names or words and ask the students how they feel about them. Return the papers to the box. Tell the class that all of the "stones" have now been put away and will not be used by anyone in the class to hurt anyone else. Make a deal that if anyone is heard using a hurtful word, he or she must write it on a piece of paper, crumple it up, and put it in the box where it can do no more harm.

Celebrate the Difference

Create a student-of-the-week bulletin board with categories such as favorite food, hobbies, pet peeves, and favorite color. Each week, choose one student to feature on the board. Have him or her make a display on the board using family photos, objects, momentos, or anything else that he or she feels represents him or her. At the end of the week, have each classmate tell one thing about the featured student that is special.

responsibility
Standing Tall

José A third-grade boy   **George** A third-grade boy

Angela A friend of José   **Tisha** A classmate of José

Renee A classmate of Jose

Ms. Lee The third-grade teacher

Jason The new boy with a slight nervous stutter

Extras Students in class and on the playground

Scene One: Mrs. Hynes's third-grade classroom.

A bell rings. Enter José, George, Angela, Renee, Tisha, and several other students. Ms. Lee enters with Jason, who stands beside her.

Ms. Lee: *(to class)* Take your seats quickly. We have a lot to do today, but before we begin, I'd like you all to meet our new student, Jason.

Tisha: Hey, Jason.

Renee: Hi, Jason.

Jason: *(shyly)* Hello.

Ms. Lee: Would anyone like to ask a question of our new class member?

George: *(raising his hand)* Where are you from?

Jason: P...P...P...Pittsburgh. *(Several students giggle.)*

José: *(raising his hand)* Do you have any brothers or sisters? *(Jason shakes his head no, but doesn't speak. He looks at Ms. Lee.)*

Ms. Lee: Okay, Jason, please take a seat behind Tisha. Tisha, raise your hand. *(Tisha raises her hand and Jason quickly sits and slumps down.)*

Fade.

     reproducible

Scene Two: The playground.

José, George, and Angela are sitting on the ground, looking at Angela's baseball cards. Their backpacks are nearby. Other students are in the background playing.

José: These baseball cards are cool. You really want to trade some?

Angela: Sure, I got a lot of new ones for my birthday and now I have a whole bunch that are alike.

George: I'll show you what I have. *(He stands, picks up his backpack, and takes out a small stack of cards.)*

Enter Jason. He is looking down and accidently bumps into George, who drops the cards.

George: Hey, look what you made me do!

Jason: I'm sorry. I'll h...h...h...help you p...p...p...pick them up.

George: *(smiling)* Say that again.

Jason: I'm sorry. *(He drops to his knees and starts picking up the cards.)*

George: Not that part, P...P...P...Pittsburgh. I mean the rest. *(Angela laughs nervously and José looks away. Jason hands the cards to George and walks toward the classroom.)*

Exit Jason.

José: That wasn't nice.

George: He bumped into me.

Angela: I think it was an accident.

George: I don't care. He made me drop my cards. *(A bell rings and George calls after Jason.)* Hey, P...P...P...Pittsburgh, you dropped your p...p...p...pencil!

Exit George. Enter Tisha and Renee.

Tisha: Why is George making fun of the new kid?

Angela: To get attention. He always picks on new kids. He thinks he's funny.

Tisha:	I'm glad I'm not the new kid.
Renee:	Somebody should tell him to stop.
Tisha:	Yeah, somebody should. Come on. The bell rang.

Exit Angela, Tisha, and Renee. José lingers for a moment in thought, then exits.

Scene Three: The classroom.

Enter George, José, Angela, Tisha, Renee, and extras. They sit at their desks. Jason enters last and quickly takes his seat.

George:	*(turning to Jason)* Hey, P...P...P...Pittsburgh, there's a spelling test today. You'll need your p...p...p...pencil. *(He waves the pencil he found in the playground. Several kids giggle. Angela looks away.)*
Jason:	Hey, that's mine.
George:	You can have it if you say please.

Jason looks at the other students. Some are smiling while others are pretending not to pay attention.

José:	Give him the pencil, George.
George:	I wasn't talking to you. It's none of your business.
José:	Yes it is. This is my classroom too, and I don't think you should be mean to Jason.
Angela:	It makes me feel uncomfortable, too. Jason, maybe I have an extra pencil.
Tisha:	I don't like it either.
George:	I was just making a joke. They laughed. *(He points to two students, who look away.)*
José:	It isn't funny. *(He turns to Jason.)* I'm sorry, Jason. This is a nice school.
Jason:	*(smiling)* I think it just got better.

Enter Ms. Lee.

Ms. Lee:	Okay class, time for our spelling test. Does everyone have a pencil? *(George hands Jason's pencil to him. José pats George on the back.)*

extension activities
for responsibility

Definition

On the chalkboard, write this definition of responsibility:

A responsible person does . . .

- think ahead.
- use self-control.
- accept responsibility for his or her own choices.
- meet his or her obligations.
- set a good example.

A responsible person doesn't . . .

- blame others.
- give up, especially when others are depending on him or her.
- look the other way if he or she can help.

Lead a class discussion on the meaning of each aspect of responsibility.

Q & A

Once you have read through the play, ask your students such questions as these:

- Why didn't José say something to George when he first started picking on Jason?
- Why do you think George thinks it's funny to bully another kid?
- How would you feel if you were Jason?

Personal Responsibilities

Across the chalkboard write *home*, *school*, and *community*. Ask the students what responsibilities they think children have in each area and write their answers in the proper columns. Ask them how they feel about the items on the finished lists.

The Furry, Scaly, and Feathered

Ask how many students have pets. Ask the pet owners to explain the responsibilities they have for their pets. Have all of the students draw pictures of their pets or imagined pets and then list the things they think are important when caring for their animals. Remind the children that caring for a pet means giving the animal not only food and water but also regular attention.

Self-Control

You will need two simple puppets for this activity. Everyone gets upset or angry at some time. How a person handles anger tells a lot about his or her character. Write some possible situations on slips of paper and put them in a box. These examples will get you started:

• Another student bumps into you and causes you to drop your books.

• Your sister/brother borrows something of yours without asking.

• A classmate blames you for something you didn't do.

Put students in pairs and have each pair draw a slip. Then let the pairs use the puppets to act out positive ways of dealing with the situations.

The Price of Choice

Create a matching game of actions and consequences. On a 3" x 5" card, write an action such as *I watch TV instead of studying my spelling words* or *I do not wear my helmet while riding my bike.* On another card, write a consequence such as *I do not do well on the spelling test* or *I fall and get a painful bump on my head.* Create twenty such pairs. Put your students in groups of five or six. Give each group an opportunity to play the matching game and see who can do it the fastest. Once everyone has had a chance, lead a discussion about actions and their consequences.

Keep Going

Explain to your students that a person of character doesn't quit, especially if others are counting on him or her. To demonstrate the effect that quitting can have on others, choose two pairs of students and have them stand at the front of the room. Put a pile of about twenty books in front of each pair. Instruct the children to move the books as fast as they can to the back of the room, but each person can move only one book at a time. The team who moves all of the books first wins. Before they begin, choose one child to quit after carrying five books, complaining that the work is too hard. When the activity is over, ask each participant how he or she felt about the fact that one child quit. Ask how it changed the contest.

Have all of the students think of "give up" phrases. Write them on the board.

Include the following:

• It's too hard.

• I can't.

• I'm too tired.

• Who cares?

• I don't want to.

• I won't succeed anyway.

As a group, come up with positive phrases to counter the negative ones.

The Finger of Blame

Cast of Characters

Andrew A third-grade boy   **Jack** Andrew's friend
Mark Andrew's friend   **Tanya** Andrew's older sister
Mom Andrew's mother

Scene One: Kitchen of Andrew's home.
There is a birthday cake on the counter.

Enter Mom and Tanya.

Tanya: Wow, Mom! The cake is so beautiful! I'm going to have a great birthday party tomorrow.

Enter Andrew, Jack, and Mark. They are running and bumping into each other. Andrew is holding a baseball bat. Mark has a glove.

Andrew: Hi, Mom. What do we have to drink?

Mom: Slow down. I told you that there is no roughhousing allowed inside.

Mark: Wow, cake!

Tanya: Don't even think about it! That's for my party.

Jack: Am I invited?

Tanya: No way!

Jack: Good, 'cause I wouldn't want to come anyway.

Andrew and Mark laugh.

Tanya: *(whining)* Mom!

Mom: Okay, settle down. Andrew, there are plenty of cold sodas in the refrigerator. You boys can help yourselves and then go back outside. Tanya, let's go put up the decorations in the living room.

Tanya: Okay, but don't you guys touch anything.

Exit Tanya and Mom.

Mark:	That icing really does look good. She wouldn't miss just a little bit down here at the edge. *(He sticks his finger in the icing and takes a taste.)*
Andrew:	Come on. Don't do that. I'll get in trouble.
Jack:	They won't even notice. I want to try some. *(He reaches out his hand to take a taste. Andrew reaches across to stop him and the cake topples to the floor.)*
Mark:	Oh, man!
Andrew:	My mom's going to kill me!
Jack:	What are we going to do? *(There is a bark at the kitchen door.)*
Andrew:	We can go back outside to play ball and one of us can "accidently" let Chloe in.
Mark:	Okay, let's go!

Exit all.

Scene Two: The backyard.

Enter Andrew, Jack, and Mark.

Jack:	Maybe Chloe will eat all the evidence.
Mark:	What a waste. That was a really good cake. What's the matter, Andrew?
Andrew:	I was just thinking that Tanya's really excited about her birthday. I don't think my mom has time to bake another cake. This will ruin it for them.
Jack:	Yeah, but if your mom finds out that we knocked the cake over, you'll get grounded for a month. She'll probably call my mom.
Mark:	Let's not worry about it. Tanya can have a special cake next year. Let's play ball.
Andrew:	I don't feel like playing right now.
Mom:	*(from offstage)* Oh, no! Chloe, what have you done?
Jack:	Maybe we'd better be going.

Mark: See you later.

Exit Mark and Jack. Andrew waits for a moment, listening.

Tanya: (offstage) Oh, Mom, look at my cake! Chloe, you bad, bad dog!

Exit Andrew.

Scene Three: Andrew's kitchen. What's left of the cake is on the floor.

Enter Andrew from stage right. Enter Mom and Tanya from stage left.

Mom: Be careful, Andrew. There's cake all over. Chloe got into the kitchen somehow and must have knocked it down. Your dad took her to the vet.

Andrew: The vet? Why?

Tanya: It was a chocolate cake, Andy. Chocolate is very bad for dogs. She ate a lot of it and might get sick.

Mom: I can't believe Chloe would do such a thing. She's usually so good.

Andrew: (softly) She didn't do it.

Mom: What?

Andrew: She didn't knock it over, Mom. I did. I was goofing around with Jack.

Tanya: You did this?

Andrew: I tried to blame it on Chloe. Now she's sick and Tanya's party is ruined. I'm so sorry. What can I do?

Mom: I'm glad you told me the truth. I'm sure Chloe will be alright. Her tummy might feel a little upset for a day or two. I think I can get another cake at the bakery. It would be fair, Andrew, if you paid for it with your allowance.

Andrew: I will. And I think I'll have to buy something else.

Tanya: What's that?

Andrew: A dog treat for Chloe.

Fade.

extension activities
for fairness

Definition

On the board, write this definition of fairness:

A fair person does . . .

- play by the rules.
- take turns and share.
- get the facts before making up his or her mind.

A fair person doesn't . . .

- blame others unjustly.
- take advantage of others.
- play favorites.

Lead a class discussion on the meaning of each aspect of fairness.

Q & A

Once you have read through the play, ask your students to answer such questions as these:

- Why did Andrew try to blame Chloe for something that he did?
- Was Andrew's punishment fair?

Playing by the Rules

Work outside, or clear a space at the front of the room. Place two empty boxes a few feet apart. Put a ball, a block, or a rolled-up piece of paper between the boxes. Choose eight students to play and tell them that the object of the game is to get the ball into a box. Have them begin. It's likely that they will be confused or that a few students will take over. Next, have the same students play the game following a few rules. Form two teams of four, with one team on each side of a box, and tell the teams they must get the ball into the opposite box. You might say that they can only touch the ball with their elbows. Add a few rules against pushing and the like. Have them begin. Ask how following the rules improved the play.

Making It Work

Explain that the way to be fair to people who disagree with each other is to find a compromise. Suggest several situations such as these:

- One student is cold and wants the window closed. The other is warm and wants it open.
- Three friends are having pizza together. There are eight pieces of pizza.
- One student accepted a friend's invitation to go swimming. Now the friend has decided that he or she wants to watch TV.

Have the students brainstorm to come up with compromises for each situation.

Equality

Bring in enough cookies for the entire class, but only pass out half of them. Tell those who get cookies not to eat them yet. Ask your students to raise their hands if they think the situation isn't fair. Ask the students who didn't get cookies how they feel about the situation. Ask how those who did get a cookie feel. Ask the students who got a cookie to think of ways to correct the situation. Use one of their solutions to make the situation fair. Then bring out the rest of the cookies and let the students divide them fairly.

The Meaning of Fair

Tell your students that fair doesn't always mean equal. Ask the student to raise their hands if . . .

- they have a bedtime earlier than that of older siblings or that of their parents.
- they have been to a birthday party where the birthday girl or boy got all the presents.
- they have had to do chores while a sick sibling was allowed to rest.

Ask the students whether each of the situations is fair and why.

You Can't Tell a Book

Bring in a magazine photo of a child. Have each student write a paragraph about the child in the picture. Instruct the students not to write about what the child looks like, but about what kind of person the child is. Read some of the paragraphs in class so your students can see how different people can get different impressions. Explain that it is impossible to know someone based on how he or she looks on the outside. Instead, we should base our opinions on the things that the person does or says.

Fairness Banner

Roll out a long piece of butcher paper and write *FAIRNESS* on it in open block letters. Around the word, let the students write and draw their feelings about fairness. Pictures might include children sharing and taking turns. Display the banner in your classroom or in the hallway.

A New Friend

Cast of Characters

Jessica A third-grade girl   **Dad** Jessica's father
Raoul Brandon's friend   **Mom** Jessica's mother
Mrs. Poe Jessica's elderly neighbor
Brandon Jessica's older brother, a fourth grader

Scene One: Jessica's front yard. Next door is a flower garden which belongs to Mrs. Poe.

Enter Mrs. Poe. She waters her flowers, then exits. Enter Jessica, Brandon, and Raoul. Jessica is carrying a Frisbee.

Brandon: *(lazily tossing the Frisbee to Raoul)* I wish we could go to the pool.

Jessica: I know it's hot, but Mom said we have to wait until Dad gets home.

Raoul: *(lightly tossing the Frisbee to Jessica)* I hope he gets here soon.

Enter Mrs. Poe.

Mrs. Poe: *(in a harsh tone)* You kids be careful with that thing. I don't want it ending up in my flower beds.

Jessica: We'll be careful.

Exit Mrs. Poe.

Raoul: Boy, your neighbor sure is grumpy all the time.

Brandon: Yeah, and all she ever does is dig around in that garden.

Jessica: *(gently tossing the Frisbee to Brandon)* I think those flowers are the only things she likes.

Brandon: She sure doesn't like us. *(He tosses the Frisbee a little too hard to Raoul, who misses it. He trips and falls at the edge of the garden, crushing a few small plants.)*

Enter Mrs. Poe.

Mrs. Poe:	*(angrily)* That does it! You three aren't going to make a mess out of my garden. *(She picks up the Frisbee.)* I'll just put this where it can't do any more harm.

Exit Mrs. Poe, carrying the Frisbee.

Raoul:	Gee, I didn't mean to hurt her dumb flowers.
Jessica:	Maybe we should go inside to wait for Dad. It's hot out here anyway.

Exit all.

Scene Two: Jessica's living room.

Enter Dad, carrying a newspaper. He sits, opens the paper and begins to read. Enter Mom, Jessica, and Brandon.

Mom:	*(to Dad)* Good morning, dear. Is there any interesting news?
Dad:	The weather is going to stay hot and dry. We sure could use rain.
Mom:	I heard something sad this morning. Mrs. Poe fell and hurt her leg. She will be in the hospital for at least a week.
Brandon:	Now maybe we can go outside without getting yelled at.
Mom:	Don't be too hard on her. She's all alone. I never see anyone visit her. Sometimes lonely people can be cranky.
Dad:	*(standing)* Well, if we are going to get to the beach today, we'd better get ready.
Jessica:	We're all ready. We'll meet you outside.

Exit all.

Scene Three: Jessica's front yard.

Enter Brandon and Jessica.

Brandon:	It sure is hot. I can't wait to get to the beach.
Jessica:	*(looking at Mrs. Poe's garden)* Look, the flowers are drooping. Mrs. Poe must not have anyone to take care of them while she's gone. We could water them.

Brandon: She'll get upset when she gets back if we mess with her garden.

Jessica: It will die if we don't. Come on. It will only take a few minutes a day.

Brandon: *(smiling)* Okay, but if we get into trouble, remember it was your idea. *(Brandon picks up a hose and waters the flower bed while Jessica uses a watering can and takes care of some potted plants.)*

Jessica: There, that didn't take long. Now let's go see if we can get Mom and Dad to hurry up.

Exit all.

Scene Four: Jessica's living room one week later.

Enter Jessica and Brandon just as the doorbell rings.

Jessica: I'll get it. *(Looking through the peephole first, she opens the door.)*

Enter Mrs. Poe. She is walking with a cane and holding a package.

Mrs. Poe: Hello, children. I'll bet you're surprised to see me here.

Brandon: Uh, yeah. How are you?

Mrs. Poe: Much better, thank you. Though while I was in the hospital, I worried every day about my garden. When I came home and saw that it was all right, I thanked your mother. But she said it was you two who took care of it. I've brought you a little something to say thank you. *(She hands the package to Jessica.)*

Jessica: You're welcome. We liked taking care of it. *(She opens the package and pulls out a new Frisbee.)*

Brandon: Cool! Thanks.

Mrs. Poe: I've been too harsh with you children. I would like to change that. Maybe when my leg is better, you could teach me to use that thing.

Jessica: *(smiling)* We'd be happy to, Mrs. Poe.

extension activities
for caring

Definition

On the board, write this definition of caring:

A caring person does . . .

• behave kindly towards others.

• consider the feelings of others.

• think about how his or her behavior affects others.

• do good without thought of reward.

A caring person doesn't . . .

• forget to give praise or gratitude.

• refuse to forgive.

Lead a class discussion on the meaning of each aspect of caring.

Q & A

Once you have read through the play, ask your students to answer such questions as these:

• Do you think Mrs. Poe was a mean person? Why did she yell at the children?

• How would the story have been different if Brandon and Jessica hadn't helped out?

Good News

Create a bulletin board for good news. Ask your students to look through newspapers and magazines and bring in pictures of people helping other people or animals. Set aside a special time once a week (or every day!) to have a student read a short, true story about caring people. Such stories can be found in magazines and newspapers or can be transcribed from television news stories.

Thank You

A caring person also knows how to express gratitude. Lead a class discussion on the meaning of gratitude. Challenge each student to design a card for someone who has helped him or her in some way. Inside the card, have the student write a personal note of thanks and sign his or her name.

Caring for Others

Have your students bring in suggestions for a class project aimed at helping someone in the community. For example, the students might write cards to people in a retirement home or to children in a hospital. Another possibility is collecting used toys in good condition to donate to needy children.

A Loving Friend

Read aloud *The Giving Tree* by Shel Silverstein (HarperCollins, 1964). Ask your students to list the ways that the tree cared for the boy. Have them think of ways the boy could have cared for the tree. Create a bulletin board with a large class "giving tree" in the center. Cut out circles of paper to represent the fruit of the tree. On each circle, have a student draw a picture of someone behaving in a caring way. Hang the fruit on the tree for all to see.

Manners Count

When you use good manners, you show others that you care. Write examples of good manners on slips of paper. Create enough for every class member. Here are some examples:

- Cover your mouth when you sneeze.
- Say thank you.
- Answer the telephone politely.
- Clean up any mess you make.
- Ask before taking something.

Have each student draw a slip of paper and then think of why using such manners shows that you care about others.

Helping Hands

Make a photocopy of a child's hand. Then make additional copies from the first copy and cut them out. When a child behaves in a caring manner toward you or his or her classmates, have the child sign his or her name on a hand and hang it somewhere in the room. Tell the students that you would like to see the helping hands stretch all the way around the room before the school year is over. If you don't have access to a photocopy machine, trace a child's hand onto construction paper and cut it out.

The Natural World

Caring for others can also include caring for animals and the environment. Ask your students to come up with ways to help the natural world. Start with these examples:

- Make and hang bird feeders.
- Create a class garden.
- Clean up trash outdoors.

citizenship
ooooooooooo

The Gift

Cast of Characters

Anna A third-grade girl
Becky Anna's friend
Hank A classmate of Anna

Mom Anna's mother
Yolanda Anna's friend
Joel A classmate of Anna

Old Woman An elderly lady in the park

Scene One: In front of school.

Enter Mom, Anna, and Becky. Mom is pushing a stroller with Anna's baby brother inside. Other students walk by on their way to school.

Mom: Okay, you two. Ryan and I will meet you right here after school. Then we can go to the park.

Exit Mom with stroller.

Becky: Your mom is really nice. Have you gotten her a present yet for Mother's Day? I got my mom some bath salts.

Anna: No. I don't have much money.

Becky: Wow, what are you going to do?

Enter Joel, Hank, and Yolanda.

Joel: Do about what?

Anna: About Mother's Day. It's Sunday and I haven't gotten my mom anything. Do you have any ideas?

Yolanda: I got my mom some candy. She always shares it with me. It's fun.

Hank: I got my mom a fancy card. She always saves them.

Joel: I haven't gotten anything for my mom yet, either. But my dad is taking me shopping after school. We'll buy something then. Hey, Hank! Look. There's no one playing with the tetherball. Come on.

Exit Hank and Joel.

Anna:	I don't have enough money to buy my mom a present. And I don't want Dad to buy it for me. Then it's from him, not me.
Yolanda:	Maybe you could earn extra money by doing some chores.
Becky:	There isn't enough time to do that. Don't worry, Anna. We'll think about it some more at the park. Do you want to go with us, Yolanda?
Yolanda:	Sure, but now we should get to class.

Exit all.

Scene Two: A play area at the park.

Enter Mom with stroller, Anna, Becky, and Yolanda.

Mom:	Ryan and I will be right over there on that bench (*she points offstage*). You all have fun.

Exit Mom.

Becky:	Have you thought of anything to get for your mom?
Anna:	No. I want it to be something special.
Yolanda:	What kinds of things does she like?
Anna:	She loves flowers.
Becky:	That's it!
Anna:	What's it?
Becky:	Look over there by that bench. There are some beautiful roses.
Anna:	Do you think it would be okay if I took them? I could come tomorrow morning and pick them so they will be fresh.
Yolanda:	Why not? They'll grow back. You're not hurting anything.
Becky:	It's a great idea. There's the ice-cream truck. I have fifty cents. Let's go!

reproducible

Exit Becky and Yolanda. Anna walks to the bench next to the rose bushes. She leans over to smell them. Enter Old Woman, who stands next to the roses.

Old Woman: They are beautiful, aren't they?

Anna: Yes, they are.

Old Woman: They are like the roses that grew near my home when I was a child. They remind me of my mother.

Anna: *(looking thoughtful)* Do you come here a lot?

Old Woman: Every day. Look, there is a honeybee on that flower. Honeybees come here every day, too. They must like the roses as much as we do.

Becky: *(offstage)* Come on, Anna.

Anna: I have to go. Bye.

Exit Anna stage left. Exit Old Woman stage right.

Scene Three: Anna's living room, the following Sunday.

Enter Mom with a cup of tea. She sits down. Enter Anna. She is holding something behind her back.

Anna: Happy Mother's Day! I have a surprise for you.

Mom: Oh, my! What is it?

Anna: *(taking out a hand-drawn picture of some roses from behind her back)* I made it myself.

Mom: Oh, Anna! It's beautiful! How did you paint such lovely roses?

Anna: Let's go to the park later and I'll show you the real roses I made the picture from. I know someone else who will be there enjoying them.

Mom: I would like that a lot *(hugging Anna)*. This is the best Mother's Day ever.

extension activities
for citizenship

Definition

On the chalkboard, write this definition of citizenship:

A good citizen does . . .

* cooperate with others.
* obey just laws and rules.
* volunteer in the community.
* protect the environment.

A good citizen doesn't...

* think only of himself.
* act disrespectfully toward people in authority.

Lead a class discussion on the meaning of each aspect of citizenship.

Q & A

Once you have read through the play, ask your students to answer such questions as these:

* If Anna had cut the roses, how would the old woman have felt when she came to see them?
* In what ways does a good citizen help to care for parks and other public places?

Stay Informed

Bring a newspaper to class. Note two or three articles that would be of interest to your students. Explain that part of being a good citizen is learning about what is going on in the local community and the world. Read the articles that you had noted. Ask if there are other ways to get information. List the responses on the board. Tell the students that you want them to bring in information that might be interesting to the class. They may get their information from sources such as newspapers, magazines, television, or radio.

Great Words

Tell your students a little about Martin Luther King Jr. Then read this quote:

> Anyone can be great, because anyone can serve.
>
> —Martin Luther King Jr.

Ask your students what they think Dr. King meant. Then ask what are some of the ways that children can serve the community. Create a bulletin board titled "KIDS CAN" and devote it to articles about children who have made a difference.

There Go the Rules

A good citizen obeys just rules and laws. Have each student write a short story about a town in which there are no laws. Tell them to imagine what it would be like to try to cross the street or park a car. Ask if they would feel safe.

What Is Just?

In class read *The Drinking Gourd: A Story of the Underground Railroad* by F. N. Monjo (Harper, 1970). Tell your students that sometimes laws may be unjust. Ask how the boy and his father in the book showed good character even though they were disobeying the law. Explain to the students that there are ways that a good citizen deals with unjust laws, such as staying informed, taking the time to vote, and, when necessary, protesting peacefully.

Rights and Wrongs

Explain to your students that citizens have certain rights, but that a good citizen does not insist on rights that would harm others. Tell the class that a famous man named Oliver Wendell Holmes once said that freedom of speech does not give one the right to yell "Fire!" in a crowded theater. Ask your students how yelling "Fire!" might be harmful to others. Suggest other scenarios such as these:

• Throwing litter out of a car window

• Letting your dog run loose in the street

• Racing your bike down a busy sidewalk

Ask how such behaviors might be unfair to other citizens.

Caring For the Planet

A good citizen protects the environment. Help your class set up a local project to benefit the environment, such as developing a recycling center at school. If you would prefer a more global undertaking, The Children's Rainforest is an ongoing project to save the rainforest in Costa Rica. For more information contact the project at this address:

The Children's Rainforest
P.O. Box 936
Lewiston, ME 04240
(207) 784-1069
(207) 777-1370

character counts!^{SM}

ooooooooooo ooooooooo

The Cap

Cast of Characters

Peter A third grader
Adam Peter's friend
Will Peter's classmate
Dad Peter's father

Darryl Peter's friend
Suzanne Peter's friend
Mr. Stone The school custodian
Extras Students in line for the bus

Scene One: In front of the school.

Extras are waiting for the bus that will take them on field trip to the zoo. Enter Peter, Darryl, Adam, and Suzanne. Peter is wearing a team baseball cap.

Suzanne: I can't wait to get to the zoo. My mom said there's a new baby tiger and two baby giraffes.

Peter: My favorite zoo animals are the alligators.

Adam: They're no fun. They just lie there in the water.

Darryl: Hey, Peter. Where did you get that neat cap?

Peter: My dad got it for me at the baseball game last week. It's a real team cap.

Adam: I'd like to have one, but I think they're expensive.

Suzanne: Here comes the bus. Let's go.

Exit all.

Scene Two: In front of the school after the field trip.

Enter extras, Darryl, Adam, Suzanne, and Peter.

Adam: You were right about those alligators. It was so cool when the zookeeper fed them. I've never seen so many teeth!

Suzanne: I still liked the babies best.

Darryl: Peter, where's your cap? *(Peter touches his head.)*

Peter: Uh oh, I don't know. I must have left it at the zoo.

reproducible

Suzanne: Maybe somebody found it. You can check the Lost and Found tomorrow.

Peter: I hope it's there.

Exit all.

Scene Three: The next day at the school Lost and Found.

Enter Mr. Stone, Peter, and Darryl.

Mr. Stone: This is everything that I have. If someone brought something back from the zoo it would be in here. You're welcome to look through it.

Peter: Thanks. *(Both boys start to rummage through the box.)*

Darryl: Hey, look! Here it is! *(Darryl pulls out a cap and hands it to Peter.)*

Peter: All right! *(He looks at the cap and his smile fades.)* This isn't mine.

Darryl: What do you mean?

Peter: I had my name in my cap. There's no name in this one, just a red mark.

Darryl: It's like yours. Why don't you just keep it?

Peter: Well . . .*(pausing, then putting on the cap)* Thanks, Mr. Stone. I found it.

Exit Peter and Darryl.

Scene Four: On the playground at lunch.

Enter Darryl, Adam, Suzanne, and Peter.

Suzanne: I'm glad you found your cap, Peter.

Peter: Yeah, so am I. My dad was disappointed that I had lost it.

Enter Will.

Adam: Hi, Will. We're going to play soccer. Do you want to play with us?

Will:	Sure. Cool cap, Peter. I had one just like it, but I lost it on the playground a couple of days ago.
Peter:	Did you have your name in it?
Will:	No, just a red mark. *(Peter looks at Darryl.)*
Peter:	*(taking off the hat)* Then I guess this is yours. I got it in the Lost and Found. Mine must be lost for good.
Will:	Wow, thanks! I hope you find yours.
Darryl:	Do you still want to play soccer?
Peter:	Sure. Let's go.

Exit Suzanne, Adam, and Will. Darryl holds Peter back.

Darryl:	Why did you tell him it was his cap? He never would have known.
Peter:	I know. But I would have, and that just wouldn't feel right.

Exit Peter and Darryl.

Scene Five: Peter's living room at home.

Enter Peter. He puts his backpack down and sits on the couch. Enter Peter's dad.

Dad:	Hi, sport. How was school?
Peter:	It was okay, but I still didn't find my cap.
Dad:	Well, *(pulling out an envelope and handing it to Peter)* maybe this will make you feel better.
Peter:	*(opening the envelope)* All right! Tickets to next weekend's game!
Dad:	I'm not promising to buy you a new cap.
Peter:	That's okay, Dad. Going to the game with you is even better.

Fade.

extension activities
for CHARACTER COUNTS!^{SM}

The Six Pillars of Character^{SM}

On the chalkboard, review the Six Pillars of Character:

• Trustworthiness

• Respect

• Responsibility

• Fairness

• Caring

• Citizenship

Have the students try to list as many of the different aspects of each as possible. As an assignment, have each student write a short poem to demonstrate an aspect of good character.

Q & A

Once your class has read through the play, ask the students to answer such questions as these:

• Why would it make Peter feel bad to keep the cap?

• Should Peter have taken the cap at all?

For Example

One of the best ways to teach good character is to model it. Ask each student to choose a person whom he or she considers a good role model. It may be a family member, teacher, community member, or celebrity. Ask the students to explain why they chose the people they did. If possible, have them bring in pictures of the people and display the photographs on the bulletin board.

It's Good to Be Me

Give each student a few minutes to think about his or her strongest character trait and write it at the top of a sheet of paper. Below that, have each child write the traits he or she would like to work on. When the students are finished, tell them to keep the papers somewhere where they will see them every day. Explain that this paper is each student's "personal mission statement."

For All to See

Create a bulletin board to display examples of good character. Ask your students to observe others in the school environment. When a student feels someone has done something that shows good character, have the student write the person's name on a 3" x 5" card and draw a picture of the incident. Display the cards and pictures on the board with a title such as "I Spy Good Character!"

Working Together

A person of character cooperates with others to accomplish mutual goals. Have your students pair up for these hands-on experiences in cooperation:

• Place a tennis ball on the floor and an empty box a few feet away. Give each pair two sticks (drumsticks, dowels, chopsticks). Have the partners face each other and both hold the ends of both sticks. Using this set-up, they must get the tennis ball into the box.

• Have the partners place a basketball between them and hold it in place with their tummies (no hands). The object is to get the basketball from one end of the room to the other without dropping it.

• Have two students stand side by side. Tie one leg of one student to one leg of the other student at the ankle. Give the partners a ball and have them try to get it from one end of the room to the other using only the feet that are tied together.

Any of these activities can be lots of fun and very active, so allow for some noise.

show time!

Raise the Curtain

You're finally ready. The actors have rehearsed and the stage is set. Now is the time to go over your last minute checklist.

- Are the costumes ready?
- Are the props in place?
- Is the stage manager familiar with any changes of scenery?
- Are the playbills prepared?
- Do you have enough seating for your audience?
- Who will turn the lights on or off if necessary?
- If you choose to serve refreshments, do you have enough?
- Do you have a camera ready to record the big day?
- Have you allowed enough time at the end of the performance for cast and crew to be acknowledged?

A Note About Props and Scene Changes

You can be as creative as you like in staging your play, but props and costumes don't have to be fancy. For example, in *A New Friend,* the flower garden can be represented by a large square of butcher paper with flowers drawn on it. In *The Gift,* Anna's baby brother can be a doll.

Scene changes can be accomplished by changing a backdrop or a few props.

Last Minute Stage Fright

Let the cast and crew know that neither you nor the audience requires perfection, simply their best efforts. Assure them that you will be on the sidelines with a script to prompt anyone who forgets a line. Be flexible. Explain that the lines don't have to be delivered word for word and real actors sometimes make mistakes and recover by improvising a little. Remind them that the point is to have fun.

Create an atmosphere of comfort. Be sure the students are not rushed and that they are comfortable in their costumes and settings.

Cast Party

An important part of any play is the cast party. It's a well-earned chance for everyone to give a sigh of relief and talk about the play. Be sure to ask the students what they learned and what they felt were the play's strongest points. Ask what they might change in a future performance. If possible, run a video of the play just for fun.

To help everyone relax, provide some light snacks and juice. Take the opportunity to hand out the participation certificates provided at the back of the book and offer praise for everyone's contribution. Have the entire cast and crew take a bow for a job well done.

A Final Word

These plays have been designed to support a program of character education. The impact of the lessons will be greatest if you follow these guidelines:

- Be consistent. Don't lower your expectations based on the situation. A person of character makes the correct moral choices even when it is difficult or costly to do so.

- Remember that your students learn a great deal from your example.

- Be specific. Try to relate the plays and activities to the students' own environment. Talk to them about situations that they have faced themselves.

- Be creative. Watch for situations that may help to reinforce the lessons you are trying to teach.

you're invited!

_____

A performance based on one of the Six Pillars of Character^{SM}

Performed by_____

School_____

Room_____

Time_____

Place_____

CHARACTER COUNTS!

JOSEPHSON INSTITUTE OF ETHICS _{SM}

TRUSTWORTHINESS • RESPECT
RESPONSIBILITY • FAIRNESS
CARING • CITIZENSHIP

certificate of
participation

Awarded to_____

On this_____day of_____

For participation in _____

Signed_____

CHARACTER COUNTS!

JOSEPHSON INSTITUTE OF ETHICS SM

TRUSTWORTHINESS • RESPECT
RESPONSIBILITY • FAIRNESS
CARING • CITIZENSHIP

reproducible